To Lucy and Benjamin ~ **Remi**

For Nina and Paloma ~ **Tonia**

First North American edition 2023

Published in 2023 by Berbay Publishing Pty Ltd
PO Box 133
Kew East
Victoria 3102 Australia

Text © Remi Kowalski
Illustrations © Tonia Composto

Publisher: Nancy Conescu
Designer: Mika Tabata
Printed by Everbest Printing

Cataloguing-in-publication data is available
from the National Library of Australia
https://catalogue.nla.gov.au

ISBN 978-1-9226106-0-7
Visit our catalog at www.berbaybooks.com

All About the

HEART

written by
Dr. Remi Kowalski

illustrated by
Tonia Composto

BERBAY
PUBLISHING

Hearts mean love, but they also mean life.

Your heart is one of the most important parts of your body.
It sits in the **middle** of your chest.

When people hug, it's a bit like touching their hearts together.

But your heart also has a **job** to do. It pumps blood around your body, giving energy to all of your muscles and other organs.

Almost every creature has a heart.

Humans, mammals, birds, reptiles, amphibians, and insects all have hearts.

Some creatures even have more than one heart—like octopuses,
who have **three**, hagfish, who have four, and earthworms, who have **five**!

But there are some animals that **don't** have one—like jellyfish and starfish!

Hearts come in all different sizes.

The smallest heart belongs to the fairyfly.
It is so small you need a microscope to see it!

I'M SO SMALL

WOW!

The largest heart belongs to the
largest animal —**the blue whale**.

A blue whale's heart weighs up to **1100 pounds**

IT'S HUGE!

and is as tall as a human adult!

OH!

OMG!

NO WAY!

Your heart is about the same size as your hand balled into a fist, and it grows with you just like the rest of your body.

It's protected by a cage.

Your heart and lungs, which make you breathe,
are pretty soft, so they need protection (as does your brain).

Thankfully, your chest is surrounded by a cage of bones called your **rib cage**.

You have **twelve ribs** on each side that protect your heart and lungs.
Even if you hurt or break a rib, your heart stays safe.

So, how does it work?

Your heart works like a **pump**, but instead of water, it pumps blood.

Your blood carries all the energy and vitamins you get from your food, and all the oxygen you breathe from the air to every part of your body.

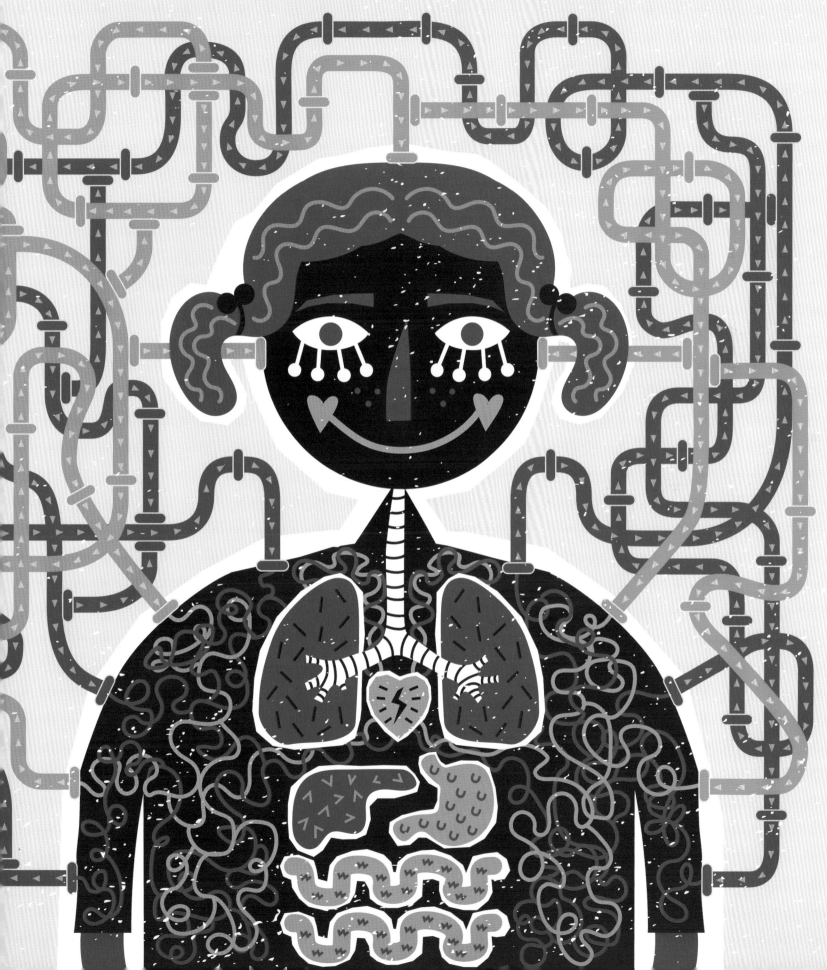

What's actually inside your heart?
Four chambers or two chambers?

Think of chambers as being like containers. They receive blood from one place and send it on to where it needs to go.

Mammals, like humans, and birds have hearts with **four chambers**. Two collecting chambers on the top called atria and two pumping chambers on the bottom called ventricles.

Not all animals have hearts with four chambers, though.
Reptiles and amphibians have hearts with three chambers
(two collecting chambers and only one pump).

3 chambers

Fish have hearts with only two chambers, and although the earthworm
has five hearts, each one has only one chamber!

2 chambers

Fun Fact

Did you know that the
picture of a love heart that
we all know so well actually
looks like a snake heart
with three chambers, not
like a human one with four!

Where does all of the blood go?

Remember how your heart has **four chambers**?
They each have an important role to play.

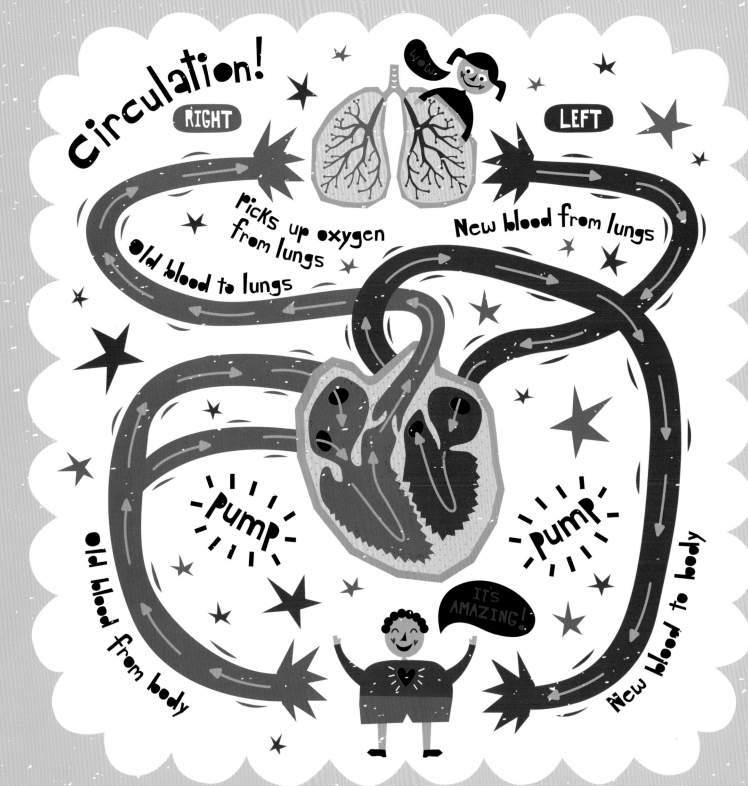

The old blood from the body comes back to the right collecting chamber and is pumped by the right pump to the lungs. Then the fresh blood full of oxygen comes back from the lungs to the left collecting chamber, before being pumped by the **left pump around the body again**.

Your heart has **four valves** inside it as well. Valves are like doors, but they only open one way to make sure the blood can only go in the right direction!

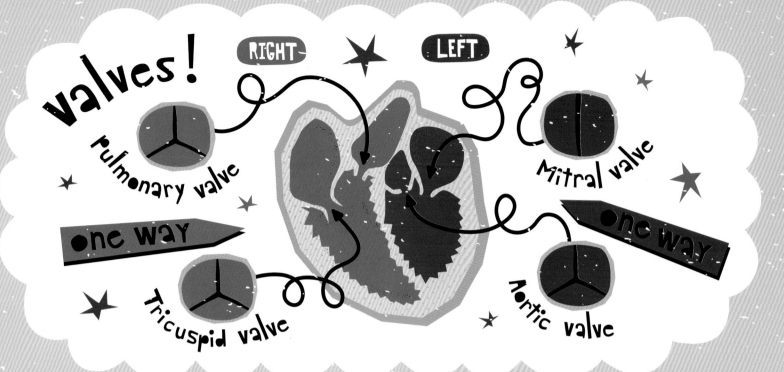

valves!

RIGHT   LEFT

Pulmonary valve

Mitral valve

one way

Tricuspid valve

Aortic valve

one way

The tubes that carry the fresh blood out of the left side of your heart are called **arteries**. And the tubes that bring the old blood back to the right side of your heart are called **veins**.

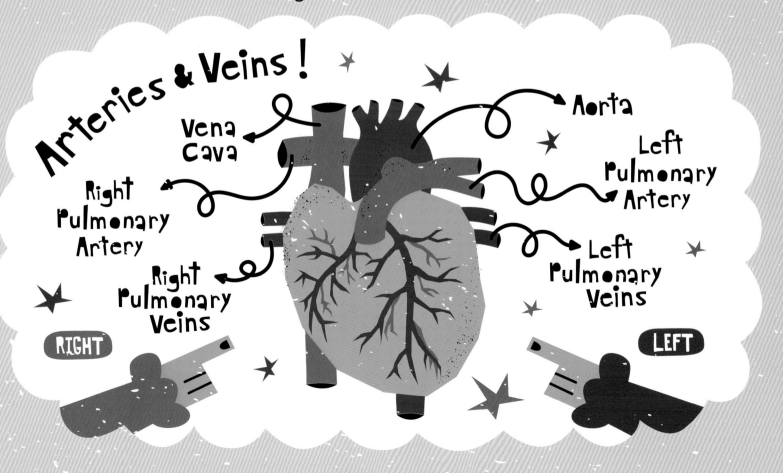

Arteries & Veins!

Vena Cava

Aorta

Left Pulmonary Artery

Right Pulmonary Artery

Left Pulmonary Veins

Right Pulmonary Veins

RIGHT   LEFT

But I thought the heart worked like a drum, too? Where's the beat?

You are right. Your heart pumps by squeezing its chambers, and it has to do this many times every minute.

TAT TAT TAT

BOOMBA BOOMBA

CHA CHA CHA CHA

EEEEE AWWW EEEEE AWWW

In an adult, the heart squeezes once every second or so, and in a child it squeezes **100 times** per minute, almost **150,000** times per day!

In an elephant, the heart squeezes **30** times every minute,
but in a pygmy shrew it beats **1500** times per minute.

You can feel the rhythm of your heart by checking your pulse—on the thumb side
of the inside of your wrist. Each little beat you feel is one squeeze of your heart.

Why do people always listen to it?

We can listen to a person's heart with a **stethoscope** and hear how the blood is flowing around it, and whether it has a good rhythm.

This can help us to figure out if the heart is healthy.

Is the heart where we feel things, too?

Because your heart is in the center of your chest, it is right in the **middle** of your body. Sometimes when you feel something very strongly, it can seem like you feel it in your heart.

But your heart doesn't actually make you feel things, because your thoughts and feelings come from your brain.

Can it really break?

Your heart can't really break in two like in the picture you may have seen of a broken heart. But like other parts of your body, it can get sick.

Hmmmm

The heart muscle can get weaker when you are old, the arteries can get blocked, or the valves inside the heart can get too leaky or too tight.

Thankfully, **doctors** have many ways to help your heart if it does ever become sick, using medicines, operations, and sometimes even special machines.

How do you take care of it?

It is very easy to take care of your heart—by eating healthy food, drinking water and getting lots of exercise.

These are things that many kids do already.

Going to visit your family doctor also helps
to ensure your body stays in good shape.

Does your heart ever take a break?

Some people think your heart stops when you sneeze
—this is not actually true.

AAAACHOOO

But your heart rhythm does speed up and slow down
all the time, even just when you breathe in and out.

Some people can even train themselves to slow down how often their heart beats if they need to keep very, very still!

What does it do when you run?

When you exercise, your muscles need much more energy, which means your heart has to pump more often (faster) and it also has to pump stronger.

Children's hearts are best at pumping very fast to help with exercise, and athletes' hearts are best at pumping more powerfully than others.

Your heart can work **five times** harder than normal to help you keep up with your friends when you are running.

But what happens when it really stops?

If your heart really stops, ambulance workers, nurses, and doctors can try to start it again for you.

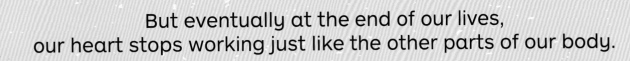

But eventually at the end of our lives,
our heart stops working just like the other parts of our body.

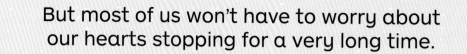

But most of us won't have to worry about
our hearts stopping for a very long time.

The heart is an amazing part of your body.
Don't forget to take care of yours. It's working really hard for you.

And next time you give someone a hug,
remember that you are really touching hearts with them.

GLOSSARY

Chambers: Compartments in the heart that store blood.

Atria: The top two collecting chambers of the heart.

Ventricles: The bottom two pumping chambers of the heart.

Valves: Door-like passages between the chambers of the heart that only open in one direction.

Arteries: Tubes that carry fresh blood out of the left side of your heart.

Veins: Tubes that bring old blood back to the right side of your heart.

Aorta: The largest artery.

Vena Cava: The largest vein.